Among Elms, in Ambush

Among Elms, in Ambush

by

Bruce Weigl

AMERICAN READER SERIES, NO. 37
BOA EDITIONS, LTD. ⁓ ROCHESTER, NY ⁓ 2021

First Edition
21 22 23 24 7 6 5 4 3 2 1

For information about permission to reuse any material from this book, please
contact The Permissions Company at www.permissionscompany.com or e-mail
permdude@gmail.com.

Publications by BOA Editions, Ltd.—a not-for-profit corporation
under section 501 (c) (3) of the United States Internal Revenue
Code—are made possible with funds from a variety of sources,
including public funds from the Literature Program of the
National Endowment for the Arts; the New York State Council
on the Arts, a state agency; and the County of Monroe, NY.
Private funding sources include the Max and Marian Farash
Charitable Foundation; the Mary S. Mulligan Charitable Trust;
the Rochester Area Community Foundation; the Ames-Amzalak
Memorial Trust in memory of Henry Ames, Semon Amzalak, and Dan Amzalak;
the LGBT Fund of Greater Rochester; and contributions from many individuals
nationwide. See Colophon on page 148 for special individual acknowledgments.

Cover Design: Sandy Knight
Interior Design and Composition: Richard Foerster
BOA Logo: Mirko

BOA Editions books are available electronically through BookShare, an online
distributor offering Large-Print, Braille, Multimedia Audio Book, and Dyslexic
formats, as well as through e-readers that feature text to speech capabilities.

Library of Congress Cataloging-in-Publication Data

Names: Weigl, Bruce, 1949–
Title: Among elms, in ambush / by Bruce Weigl.
Description: First edition. | Rochester, NY : BOA Editions, Ltd., 2021. |
  Series: American reader series ; no. 37 |
Identifiers: LCCN 2021009567 (print) | LCCN 2021009568 (ebook) | ISBN
  9781950774418 (paperback) | ISBN 9781950774425 (ebook)
Classification: LCC PS3573.E3835 A823 2021 (print) | LCC PS3573.E3835
  (ebook) | DDC 818/.5408—dc23
LC record available at https://lccn.loc.gov/2021009567
LC ebook record available at https://lccn.loc.gov/2021009568

BOA Editions, Ltd.
250 North Goodman Street, Suite 306
Rochester, NY 14607
www.boaeditions.org
A. Poulin, Jr., Founder (1938–1996)

*for Zora Dorothy Grasa Weigl and Albert Louis Weigl,
and for Chieko Kondo, in memoriam*

Contents

Part II: Razor

Part III: The Name of Beauty on Ngô Quyền Street

The God-fugitive is now too plainly known.
—Herman Melville, *Moby Dick*

Part I:

The Problem with Shapes in the Night Trees

Tale of the Tortoise

I don't know how the tortoise got in through the fence and past the neighborhood dogs that run loose once the sun is down, but I found her near a nest of her eggs where the garden had already begun to turn to autumn. It seemed she'd found a home there, and who was I to tell her otherwise, so I brought her straw to make a better bed, and food I never saw her eat but that disappeared from the tin plate where I put it. I don't remember now how long it took, but she kept the eggs warm until they hatched, and her many babies scrambled out in every direction until she rounded them up again into her care. Now I have to tell you that there never was a tortoise, only one that I wanted to be there. There never was a fence to crawl under, or neighborhood dogs for someone to step around down the dark alley. There was no dark alley. There was no nest or eggs, no straw, no hope for anything. But I did find a tortoise in my yard one morning where it had laid its eggs in a nest it had made with mowed grass. I don't know where she came from but perhaps she was a neighbor's pet, and there was a zoo nearby. I called the police to see if they knew what to do, and they came quickly, and confirmed that it was a tortoise, with eggs. Sometimes you need to tell a story to fill a hole in your mind, or to try and mend something that's been torn by a violent wave that washed through you once. There was no tortoise, and no policeman. I know, I have to stop doing this. I want you to believe me. It's all about the story. It's all we have.

The Man in the Chair

The man in the chair is screaming his life away. No one cares that his bathrobe has fallen open, exposing the white skin of old age. No one cares that he's screaming until the screams float down the hallway, and then out into the night that cares even less.

The maple trees I'm watching die have so much more freedom in their dying than the man in the chair. Someone who looks like me whispers in his ear that it will be alright, but for now he doesn't stop screaming, each scream a wave that comes from far away then breaks onto our rocky shore.

I don't know if the maple trees know that they are dying. Nothing can be done, so I watch them die and trim the dying branches and carry them away. The man in the chair wants someone to carry him away. He won't stop screaming in the nursing home where my demented mother keeps her eyes closed but manages a "Shut up" on her own. This is what a life may come to after all, this is what a life is, and means, and smells and tastes and sounds like.

According to Loop Quantum Gravity Theory

Homer gives us a history of his own world. *The Iliad* shows us fifty days of a ten-year war.

Don't forget Thetis, mother of Achilles, or Artemis, sister of Apollo.

The stories were already old. A thousand years before Christ, the stories were already old, so you might ask, why our need for sacrifice, given how one thing is connected to all other things, and therefore, to everything that you can touch at least.

The gods are at work in Homer. They punish, and they reign over everyone, and they gave the Greeks a reason to be afraid. What would we call it now, this kind of god, and whom may we blame for the world's transgressions? Already we have violated even outer space, and the numbers matter, man, the math matters: you take so much out every time, until there's nothing left.

All at Once

I realize that the roses on my hotel desk are not paper as I had thought, but real, their redness blasting through the gloom. Outside,

the Hà Nội traffic breezes past. Sometimes I don't know where I am but it's not a problem really, only a slight deviation from the path. I used to keep a shiny stone in my pocket to hold in my hand at times like this because I thought the stone was always in the world. I was wrong about a lot of things in those days. I want to go back

to the roses on my desk because the nature of their beauty is almost too much to bear, and they are not paper as I had thought, and the room is not a hole I fell into in the green place, and the bed is not my bunker. I love the mottled leaves, the long stems that prick.

For Nguyên Mai

The People Have Spoken and They Are Ugly

Soon the free zones will emerge, new borders drawn in whatever blood it will take

so those of a kind can flock together beyond what they fear. You know what I mean; this could happen. The people have spoken, and they are as ugly as the lies that they told to smother freedom, but you can only change yourself to better understand their greed, you can never change the others. This happens in history, this strange swell of ignorance that comes up from some murky place in our hearts when there is a need for blood, and it will last until that need is satisfied.

The teacher says: secure the raft of life and death, but it's so hard to act without doing, to walk on paper thin as air, and never tear a single thread.

The Woman on the Train

I am waiting for the woman on the train that rolls through ancient mountains towards Lào Cai. She is riding in a sleeper car alone. She is full of many languages, as safe as she could be, her mind a star she let me see. I am waiting for the woman on the train who is tracing the scar on her face with her long fingers. I want to trace that scar which I love, with my lips. I want everything about her inside of me, like the spirit love is, raising me above the loss and sorrow into something else that feels like being free

to live under the hands of love and understanding, in a simple house with a garden, and a room to sing and dance in, oh my. I've almost reached a point of understanding the nothing that I know. I am waiting for the woman on the train that moves closer with every breath, to the thousand-year-old city that waits in the night like a hallelujah of grace, clear as the Buddha's eyes because of how she is in the world, so much her brave self, so beautiful and strong.

I Hate to Say This

When the first responders entered the room of murdered children in their school, what they heard were their cell phones ringing, each a different tone, from their pockets and their small backpacks. You know the answer. The news had already spread. The mothers and fathers could only call and hear the empty ringing. Too much lightness and hope were slaughtered away from the world that we can't even let ourselves feel. I want a wide and sweet river to wash us away to another place where the children are fucking safe from the mad shooters and the generals with bombs. It is only our will that we need to find and hold onto. Not the best tea, but vegetables with rice, water-dipped leaves, the whole of earth and sky with its emptiness. No one should have to hear that sound, ever, from either end of the long wire through space that shrinks with every dying star.

Jesus Saves and Jesus Heals

Says the sign on the pale church in the slashing Georgia sun, to the man on the motorcycle cruising Baptist back roads for whatever fix you don't want to know, the sound like the sound a century makes when it rolls over into another grim century, a human howl at night of ecstasy.

We only wanted to be free in those days, and we worshiped regret yet clung to each other at the same time, heartfelt beat of love against your ribs. Don't let the love betray you. Don't let the night's scarred face be more than it is, heartily sorry for having offended thee.

To Him, Who Is Me

It's taken so long to get to you, that I don't know if there is enough time for a life left, or a road I could walk down in the dark and be safe. How quickly under the hungry hands of sexual intruders you fled, and how beautiful your disguises all along the way of my life, never victim, always fool, until I was confirmed into another way. The deadly sniper's aim is only about breathing, the same way you survive the pressure of abuse, only by breathing your way through. You, inside the après-belt dark room, can come out. I want to see your face. I want to let you be who you are in every crevice, in every mote of dust that floats enough into sunlight to become visible and then disappear. Now that we have found each other, we have everything.

Draft of Final Chorus I

Peace is the new word that you heard, the way of things now. No more hiding in dark bunkers with ghosts who bow to their visitors, come to hide from bombs, their tombs still unprepared in the rice fields. A single new rice plant is laid down. A single new rice plant that could become the world is stuck into the muddy earth

         so everyone is hurled somehow forward in time, or this may all be a dream that the lost hold onto, so it seems they behold something when they look out across the almost empty fields, they shout to their children who play under a safe sky to come home and eat the little that they have, their eyes resting in a pool of new light,

         but this is the song of those who fled at the end of days, the helicopters hovering over the embassy like giant insects, the thousands of people fleeing in fear of what they were told, the way they would die if they stayed, losing track of the incense smoke that could show them their way back home.

Draft of Final Chorus II

No slaughter, no crimes against people who left for a country that had come to destroy them, the steeple of the pink cathedral quiet now, only fires burning in the buildings of the failed empire, to keep their secrets buried in the ashes, flashes of the final explosions lighting the sky, this is the song of the people who ran away from their own language, from the spirit kept alive for thousands of years. They could not stay.

They could not stay when they could ride the hovering helicopters away from some trouble that would never come, so the streets were almost empty for a time, the only sound some joyful celebrations, while the fleet waited at sea for the refugees who gathered around their protectors and guides to a new world as if they were brothers. Who could know how their lives would be, the old flag unfurled in a place so far away? In the snow of America, they found their new homes.

Or in the warm California sun they laid themselves down in strange beds, the quiet moans of remembering, rising like the mist, like the pealing of the bells in the pink church that were quiet now.

For Nguyen Tan

The Problem with Shapes in the Night Trees

On guard duty one night and as stoned as I could be, I took my place, mumbled to the guy I was replacing and settled into my position. The same thing was happening all up and down the perimeter so there was more noise than there should have been, but soon things quieted down and after a few more minutes I looked out at the rice fields that stretched out like a graveyard as far as I could see. I'd done this before and sometimes under much more duress, but the Việt Nam reefer had a hold of me, so I was reeling a bit, and glad I could sit down. I needed to focus so I squinted into the dark to get my night vision straight.

At first, I could only barely make out the line between where the rice fields ended, and the sky began, but as my eyes became more and more accustomed to the dark, I began to see more details. I looked and shook my head and looked again. I saw an entire platoon of Việt Cộng soldiers moving almost imperceptibly in my direction through the dark, which was everyone's direction, and my simple duty to defend, my sacred duty to defend the LZ which I did, with all of my heart. I needed to alert the guy down the line, but I couldn't see him in the dark, and I didn't want to make any noise, not a sound.

The problem with dark shapes in the night trees is that sometimes they're bodies. I squinted again into the dark rice fields and put my nose to the breeze until I saw that the Việt Cộng were water buffalo, easing through my line of fire. I could be easy as well and breathe again. But that's not the end of the story because someone down the line at three a.m. pulled his claymores when some trip flares lit up our position and I heard the sputter of rifle fire nearby, all up and down the line. As the trip flares descended among us, you could see the shapes of water buffalo in that too sharp light; here and there and then so quickly gone. A few more rounds cracked, and then it was quiet again, so I could hear a frightful bellowing coming from the darkness,

sharp cries that sounded a lot like pain to me. All I could do was stay in my position and hope whatever it was would die soon so the sound of its dying would stop, and maybe that would be the end of it for the night. It's from our links with other things that memory occurs, that's why they won't let go sometimes, no matter what you think or pray. The farmer found the bodies even before first light and dragged one calf to our bunker. Its eyes were still open, so it seemed to look at me, its stilled gaze including me in the difficulty surrounding us all. I was eighteen years old and didn't know much. I heard some voices raised in anger in the background; money was involved, and then some deals made I think, that would allow everyone safe passage out of the wreck of waste the war had become, but I wasn't thinking about that. I was thinking about the bawling sound the calf had made after being torn to shreds by the claymore when it tripped the flares in its playful romping just off some ancient path through the rice. How human the voice had sounded, and how full of longing for peace. Any kind.

Homewood Nineteen Fifty Something

Secret tests were being conducted by the government in those days. Larry Baker's father dug a bunker in his backyard one summer—bomb shelter they called it—and although we practiced hiding under our desks at school, no one knew what any of it meant. In the Nevada desert they vaporized the air and turned it into fiery dust that blew across the model towns and the model people like voracious jaws stretched open to kill and eat it all. This

was the world we were given, although we wouldn't know that for years to come. When we finally got down into Larry Baker's bomb shelter, it was mostly empty except for some candles and some food in cans no one would eat, but we loved the utter darkness once the hatch was pulled shut against the sun. Quiet, we sat there, and waited.

This Back-Porch Rocker My Prison

As if the sun was going down one last time, we are killing ourselves with desperate pleasure

so primitive, the brain will not let go once it has a taste, once it has a chance to warm up a vein, then an arm, then a whole way of being, which is a way of not being in the world.

I wonder where the love was when we needed it. I heard the lark sing out across the green expanse of time, and then I heard that song come back as if it didn't matter to the night, no souls out there to call us in return, only ourselves to hold the wall against such need as you have never seen or felt before. Leave the door open, turn the lights on and hold the child tight against you. Hold the child tight, and against you.

War Story

I'm waiting for the war to end for me. I'm waiting for the sound of rockets and mortars to stop rushing through my sleepless nights, for the crack of ambush to quiet, for the movement through the hazy trees to stop and then be nothing but sun coming up through waves of green and yellow bamboo by the river someone had fought hard to defend a thousand years before. I'm waiting for the dead to stop returning from their places in harm's way, so I won't have to care for them. I'm waiting for the war to end for me, the dreams of gunfire out of nowhere, the rounds I feel in my back going in, the faces of the enemy so near I can see the oil on their skin. Someone give me something to take or tell me something to believe or teach me something to help me forget, but we all know the truth about that now. How there is no way back from the knowing something right down to your soul, how there is no remedy for how the brain is twisted into a loop that will never end, until it does.

Miami Nights

The needle only takes and never gives. The needle takes the flesh away to salve the ancient brain through long canals of blood. The needle takes the blood away then gives it back all juiced and hot to send you into something that is never there. That's the best of it, the nothing part. Know nothing, see nothing, hear nothing, say nothing, feel nothing, be nothing, and then the car light's sudden shock through the trees between houses of a place you don't recognize anymore as your own, and you're out of that wave of a rush that will only kill you, the way the needle only takes, and never gives back.

To the Reader, on the Dharma

May I tell you that I find great comfort in the pattern of the cat's fur? We don't even know each other, so you might think that I'm weird, or crazy, when what I'm trying to talk about is the weight of sadness that we all have to carry around with us into the world and then pretend that it's not there. The black and white cat is a wonder of symmetry and symmetry gone wrong, and I love to trace the continents of white against the black sea that undulates. We don't even know each other, but I can tell you that this pattern of color across the cat's long body gives me hope; it gives me a moment of happiness, just when I need it the most, and that must be what brings us together, the way we understand how that can happen to someone in our situation. I have been here a long time, and still, I haven't found my way.

Love Letter to Myself and to Mule

I don't need your empire, but I wanted to stand inside the bright circle of the force that you are, the mind and the beauty that shines through the otherwise dark clouds. I ain't saying it's hard, my life, but I wish the fluttering wings would stop beating inside my head, and I wish the ghosts of the corner of my eye would finally give up and leave me alone. A river healed me once from moral injury. You have to stand in fast water at night to feel this, bats sometimes tipping your line in the dark.

Mourning Khâm Thiên Street

I walked through the bodies of trees in the mist of Ba Vì, some dry leaves rattling the quiet awake. Going back is a kind of mistake we make when we're desperate for some blue and clear air but going back is a needed thing too. To the place where we could not sing the buried children's cries away: "Mother, hold me out of here" defies all reason when it comes from the mouth of a child buried under the rubble of American bombs, the wild air stunned into blissful shock. Walk with me through the bodies of trees until we knock on the doors that were blown away. We came to this mountain to bow and to pray for the lost at Khâm Thiên who could never go home to houses that were only rubble, the quiet that was strange, the sky, after burning, the color of the rose.

For Lương Tử Đức, Chu Lượng and Nguyễn Quang Thiều

Saturday Night in Bangkok
with Nguyễn Thị Hạnh I

Do you know how the music of her life lives inside of a daughter from Bình Lục, Hà Nam Province of bad weather and magnificent rice, I know a small light, or a grace, when I see one. All the ages in her, all the ages in me, one river coming to another river at the muddy heart of it all.

Everywhere are Buddhas. I have stroked the seven-mile-high mountain with a silk cloth once a day until it wore away (a hundred thousand lifetimes), and I have only now begun to live, after a lesson from my daughter, in her language, the music of it, the river all through her.

Saturday Night in Bangkok
with Nguyễn Thị Hạnh II

As we are leaving the room this Sunday night in Bangkok, the girl, Nguyễn Thị Hanh, my daughter for one week, one day, who had never held in her hand or used a coin before, pointed to the Thai coins that I'd thrown onto the dresser as I do at home. And Nguyễn Thị Hạnh, from Bình Lục, proud as true grace can be, as in the lotus, as in the wind of ancestors, points to the coins and urgently tells me something I cannot understand, so I have to try and search for it in the dictionary and then translate. In this she is patient as I fumble with her words, and she points to the coins again and rakes her fingers across them and says once more, "cho những người ăn mày," *for the beggars.*

Out Here

What do you want out here? I hear the night ask when I step out for something I can't name but let's call cool air. Then the night shows me faces in places I choose not to remember in spite of medication and mental health guidance. Some doors I keep closed for everyone's sake. Yet I love to watch the garden at the end of day and hear the evening birds gather in the maples where I can take the whole world in, shadows lengthening until they change into night one more time.

Or there could be a car wreck of memory barging through all barriers with no forgiveness. Listen, it's not complicated; you are accountable for every single time you pulled the trigger, or even helped light someone up. You have to strap that on; there's no other way, the need-fires always burning in the distance, and the long-awaited screams finally arriving among us all. The wound, Rumi said, is the place where the light enters.

Travel Writing, I

Her shipwrecked eyes I'd never see again unless the rain
turned into blood. I need to hide, this curtain's not enough
to stop the buzzing metal from whizzing past my head. I'm
always never in a room I have to ask just where I'm at. The
windows will not say, although I'm not afraid. Yet stay with
me still is the feel of her hands on my back when I stood
against someone drunk and with a weapon, beating down
the other side of our door. For him, and for me, only a jungle
waited. For her, the rest of her life.

The Problem with Desire

I wanted the storm this afternoon somehow to come and be inside my body and everything I say and do. I wanted the green shock of trees in summer to fill me up, and the roots and worms and beetles underneath everything in their own webs of wonder, their own universe, to be my blood. I believe it is possible for something like this to happen, spinning as we do at the ends of sharp sticks, over the river of voices.

Après Flashback for My Good Doctor

Three crows fly past now as if showing me a way out of this. A dog barks next door. The evening trees are full of birds and birds' songs. The rain has come and gone, the air lighter. You could say that anything is possible, that the verdant neighborhood stretches as far as time, where anything can be forgiven, but the weight stays on my chest like a car engine, and the knot in my throat is tighter, and this is afterwards, after I come back from swirling through dark places. I must adore them to go there so often.

Wade Park VA

Rain slices through me as if I was the grassy field. No matter how many times you turn the key, the lock will not open. The birth of someone's hair piled high this morning on her head which she did with her only remaining arm and hand, VA hospital, Wade Park; she's here in mental health with the rest of us, as if there were answers. She could have had help tying up her hair that way, on top of her head; I don't think you can do that with only one hand, but I may be wrong. People under duress do amazing things to save themselves from oblivion. Back outside in the rain, nothing has changed. The woman who lost her arm to another war would not look up from the floor where she kept her eyes until the nurse called her name. She was tall when she stood up, and her hair was wildly trying to free itself from the bun she had tied it into so carefully in the morning. Another turn of the wheel is all, and when it comes to rest this time, someone's arm is missing, and someone else's mind.

Part II:

Razor

Sometimes How It Feels

Crucify me but don't leave me alone tonight with nothing but the data. Everyone is awakened by the loud instructions shouted over the PA system. So delightful our excesses: spring fever among the mad, auto-asphyxiation in the doorway of an old sexual pleasure, the enema bag hanging like an exposed heart against the white porcelain, but this is all ancient history. Nothing can be brought back from there.

For Doctor J.

Mourning the Postmodern

Peel a green onion like stucco, the layers, the steady rain a paradigm I could not situate because of its radiance. Later, an insect found solace on my thumb and made a triangle of its small life there. Nothing to do but wait, watch the clock, pretend that everything is fine.

Black Swans in the Garden of Perfect Splendor

Built by the emperors of the Qing Dynasty as their summer resort, Yuanmingyuan Park fell into disarray, and in 1860, Anglo-French troops sacked it and burned it to the ground. After the birth of the People's Republic, the damaged gardens were restored by local farmers. It is so beautiful and considered so important, it's now the place of the Lotus Flower Festival. I'm stalling

because the black swans are too beautiful for me to even remember, and because there is no beauty like the black swans that words could ever say. Just to think them brings their beauty back to me like a coronary shock, and I think they are the saddest things I have ever seen in this poor world, and I believe they must have come from somewhere else, black angels who descended from the clouds beyond our knowing and are now among us in such a perfection of beauty that you can hardly breathe when you see them on the lake, with their young, just at dusk, against the sun going down. Except when they lift their wings to expose the only white they carry, they are impossible to see in the dark.

For Xia Lu

Frog Melody

The frog hung onto the maple tree and sang its evening song, so it was just the two of us out there in the night, alone and trying to find a song to sing. I tried to call back to the frog through the night and thought for a moment that it heard me for the way it stopped when I clicked my tongue and lips, but it was no more than a coincidence, and it became clear that the frog paid no attention to me or to whatever sound I made, and instead was finely attuned to the only one note he hoped would come back to him through the dark avenue of trees. And what I wanted to come back to me I didn't know, although I hung my song out there too, on a wire, and hoped for the best. How many thousand years have we been doing this.

For a Friend Who Died

The possibilities are too horrible to imagine, though I know there's no other way to let you go. Right now, something is stuck inside my chest that feels like a cold steel ball pressed against my heart. I saw too many die under fire, but you were in the care of someone beautiful, who loved you, so I want to close my eyes and see you there among the warmth of love and compassion, in your own bed, in your own house which you loved, with your woman at your side until the absolute very end of things consumed you. We had laughed about this with each other one night in Atlanta, a cold drink between us, and a bowl we passed back and forth. We had bravely laughed to each other about the end, and how we had no fear except the fear for those we would leave behind, and how we were ready, anytime, for the end to come through a blue and opening sky.

My Final Job Application

I arrive at the door to this job after a long journey from the juncture of memory and imagination. Memory—the technical skills I've learned working beside some masters of our trade for several years, and imagination—embracing and sustaining it so it blossoms into colors I didn't know I knew. This is what separates the truly accomplished from the hobbyists, and I've spent the past forty years learning the complicated art of weaving those two points of view together. The goal is to find that seamlessness in language that resonates in the best of any kind of writing. If I'm right about this, I'm a good match for this position, and I'll be a fortunate addition to your team.

Where I Am When I'm Not Here

I dwell among the fragile ones when I'm not here, and Lord, they are not easy to please. They have long claws for clinging to the world, and they can't let go; besides, all the paradigms are different, so it would be impossible for me to explain it here. I'd need more time than this.

I'd have to start with the passageways through which things—I don't know what else to call them—travel from one place to another place. From their place to our place, in a sense. At least you could understand it that way. And then I'd have to tell you about how a place can be a machine inside of which you must find your way over and around sharp angles that are not built for your comfort or convenience. And there are only lights at junctures, too bright to bear, and sometimes faces flashing past very quickly and full of anguish.

Some spirits live there who don't want you around; artillery booms in the distance; small-arms fire cracks through groves of bamboo; a mine is waiting for someone's foot, but I can always find my way back to the garden where I started this, among the day lilies and among no one who wants to murder me, where I can imagine I am safe, and that the blue door of the sky is open for me to leave, anytime I want, where I am, when I'm not here.

From a Soldier's Diary

I stood a long time under shelter of the garage, the big door open like a mouth. I was watching the soaking summer rain fall so hard you could hear the voice of the water rise from the fields exactly like a mist, and the voice was inside of a song from the ancient time, when people still believed. I saw the hungry there too, as if through a dark tunnel, huddled together in their needs, ragged, tired, on the verge of a necessary ending,

and then the thunder snaps me back to the garage's open door. I'm all alone. Lightning brilliant and nearby flashes across the landscape in spidery fragments of light, and the rain continues, soaking everything in a milky haze, the branches drooping like the bodies of the very old. Like you, I wanted the rain to be only that, but I could not ignore the words the rain spun out somehow all around us, though nothing changes; empty rooms remain empty, empty beds, and an urgency of the beautiful flesh. Empty is the end of things that way.

Hà Nội Morning

Coffee on Tông Đản Street in Hà Nội and it's so hot people cover themselves with clothes. I'm watching a young boy trying to herd his grandmother's chickens back into their cage with a broom, small pearls of sweat gathering on his forehead. He laughs so hard when they refuse to go in and instead run out into the street and down the sidewalk, until his grandmother scolds him, and then she scolds the chickens too, who all dutifully file back into their cage. This pace of life feels so good to me that I could wear it like a shirt. I could lose the one person, and then find the other.

Deep Water

I am a river drowning in starlight so when you turn your face to me, your hand in mine, the burdens of the free world all fall away so there is only the necessary hurt that love can bring, all spinning in the air between us like a silver ball of ideas, like a silver light of possibility and peace. I hold you in the arms of peace. I hold you in the arms of peace, and in the arms of loyalty, like wind is loyal to the branches, like the blessed life that I have left will be loyal to you.

I prayed on top of Ba Vì Mountain and could feel your hand around mine, electric to the touch, divine, but more of the earth, your fingers planting seeds in the rich soil older than Christ. How can I see you so clearly, and what does it mean, and why has it swept me forever away? Oh, sweep me forever away. I am a paper boat on the river of your body where I drift in the dark until there is nothing left but waves of peace washing over me, and your arms wrapped around me to find me somehow after all the miles, waiting for you as I have always waited, love like light that could kill. You run through me like a river. You bury me in your deep water.

For JKW

Elegy for Lux

Sometimes there is no way to say goodbye because goodbye means letting go, and how could we let go of you. Some angels are supposed to stay with us, here on this poor world, and sing their songs so we won't be afraid of who we are. That's you now, angel Tom, as you always were, the generous spirit we needed, and once in Bronxville, we stayed up all night writing poems, saying lines back and forth then laughing so hard you'd think something dubious was happening, because it was—the horrors of poetry, raw and drunken and stoned, blared out into the apartment and out the summer open windows too. I don't know how else to see you or remember you, you sweet fucker of a poet saint.

Blowing Rock in Autumn

The mountains here are restless and seem to want to move somehow and tear themselves off their deep roots so they can drift to the horizon that has always called to them, always promised happiness and calm. I have nothing more to say about that right now because the trees are still, and empty of birds, and I'm all alone in the mountains of Blowing Rock, North Carolina. We almost know who we are, but not quite yet. What happens has already happened, and what hasn't happened will go on not happening beyond even our remembering. I can live with that, as long as I am permitted to fly up with the crows who fly in and call me to join them in their raucous bargaining through the neighborhood trees.

For Bruce Dick

Trigger

The fireflies make their own galaxy of stars, their own universe, blinking on and off in a code that calls to each other through the dark and enviable evening, until what? Even if you watch them, everywhere in the neighborhood dark with their yellow light, it doesn't mean anything about their lives. Night keeps its promise. Some heavy movement in the treeline, low branches bent and then released; was that the metal-on-oiled-metal-sound of weapons being readied? I think it was. I think there is no escape from this, doctor. No true salvation for any of us with dirty hands that way. Sorrow is a bed that you lie down in; grief is the sheet you pull over yourself against the cold.

Elegy for C.D.

It's not the end of the world, although I know it feels that way, all starlight-blind and everlasting. You are everlasting as an Ozark redwing calling out its hopeful, lonely cries as if someone were listening. No one is listening is the not-so-secret-secret leaked out into the atmosphere to make a cartoon bubble with some words written there as if under great rocks in fast water. You are fast water. You were all of Arkansas that San Francisco could take, judge's daughter, not lost in a storm but a storm yourself. Once,

in some labyrinthine abandoned rooms, we fell against each other in the not-so-fractured light, and another time, in a cold Manhattan flat, where you called me to your bed to warm me up and told me the story of the man who shot himself twice in the heart in the name of love. How great a space you leave here, I long even for your absences.

Elegy for Mahnke

I read your last words to me over and over again, but nothing happened. You didn't speak to me, and no spirit floated through the space that I occupied to let me know that you were here. What I hate is that no one knows how hard you fought, just to stay alive, and no one will ever know the innocently beautiful poems you wrote either, but what's the good in worrying about any of that, when we both agreed there were more important things than our lack of fame or fortune.

I had come from a war, and you had come from Iowa, but it was you who taught me irony. Now I wonder how far that irony would go. Is it ironic that you're dead, and I'm still alive, sitting here writing to you? Is it ironic that you left such a hole in the name of your absence that you wouldn't even believe? No, that's not what you meant. You meant something more about how warm a death can feel to a grieving body, and about how deep a friendship can run, like a river, underground. I don't even hate your death. I hate our lives without you.

The Shadow Knows

The beautiful woman in the rearview mirror is not looking back at you; she does not even see you, the shadow says to its man, who is driving back-bar streets to find someone in the rearview mirror to love, someone who would look in return; who would tell the man with her eyes what he wanted to hear and feel through his body like a snake. You're wasting our time, the shadow says. We could be at home by now, feeding the baby, or tending the garden; I noticed that the onions needed water?

The shadow says everything in such a way as to make it into a question by slightly raising the pitch of the final two syllables. In this way, he is always assured of being right. Who knows what hearts of terror live inside of men?

Small Song for Anna

Just now the shadows of trees are getting longer in the sun. There's something that I remember from a long time ago that will not free me into space until I hold it in my hands and turn it in the light to see whose pain it is.

It isn't the rain I'm waiting for any longer, but more your name, in the calligraphy of branches bent by the wind against the still gray sky of evening. I wanted to be part of the storm somehow. I wanted a different life, away from the noise and hubbub, to find peace in a small village house, woken by the chickens and by the dogs, hungry for their breakfast as the sun comes up beyond rice paddies as far as I can see. I wanted a small garden which we could tend together in the sun; I love to bring the new plants cool water, and I love to till the soil with a hoe—to turn it up, my grandmother always said.

Weather Report for Riley H.

The wind blew and blew forty miles per hour all afternoon long. The wind blew the trash away, and it blew the new flowers away, and it blew the demons down from their hiding places high in the branches, and the angels were blown away by their own wings, and the house with its people, whom the house loved but could not save, were blown away, and the congressmen were blown away from their valley of lies, and their lies were blown away and you want to turn around and say, "What the fuck is going on out there?" but the wind does not listen,

and it blows on past our wildest imaginings, until it feels like the world has been swept clean of the debris of all our wasted opportunity, and it's cooler now, by the lake.

For Heinemann

Fool That I Am

How can you send mere children into the mouth of war and expect them to come back to the same bright lights they were? Fool that I am, I'll take a single bird song through the winter trees as proof of my happiness. They have come back from their winter homes early because like the rest of us, they are confused, and it is more than the angle of light, more a feeling that something is different, that it's time to move on.

Nothing happens simply because you want it to happen, it took me way too long to realize. Prayer had gotten in the way, prayer, and the angle of repose of all the grief a killing field can bring a soul.

I'm just now back from that, *just now* meaning fifty years, and I wonder, watching the cold rain out of my window, whoever came up with the idea that we could be all right again.

Razor

An edge that you may fall over when you disconnect to see
things that is very difficult to find your way back from once
you are ready to head home. My advice to the mockingbird:
spend more time listening, hope being in such short supply,
and women, whose hair has been murdered,

now occupy the house slaves built for the president.
Permission has been granted to shoot the coyotes—they are
so fine, and so beautiful—in the suburbs, because they eat
the pets of the rich. None of this works very well, and the
killing is always sloppy, a waterfall of blood.

The New Law

The new law says the old law is wrong about being right. Is that thunder? Don't fuck with me, you mortar rounds of memory, deep in the brain. Deep in my brain is an iceberg. The new law says that on both sides of the door are liars, and that even the axe murderers should be sheltered from this storm.

Inside her face was a starry night.

Is that a mortar being walked right fucking in on us now; it sounds like a mortar being walked in from the treeline. Jagged is as jagged does. I thought those were stars in the black sky, exploding, the first time I woke from the deep sleep of exhaustion into attack, three a.m., Quảng Trị Province, shit—rockets and mortars, sappers tangled in the wire.

The new law says the old law is only a freaking thunderbolt just now through the bedroom's window, through the bunker's small opening, a shot, and a flash, then the count until it rumbles. Grant me my immunity, and I'll tell you everything; absolve me from all the bloody guilt, and I'll be just like you.

Watching My Great-Uncle Shave, Johnstown PA, Circa 1954

All hard memory revolves in fragments, my good doctor says, and the memories begun in trauma are the most shattered, like a white dinner plate thrown across the room at the antique clock on the wall.

Then the opposite must be true as well, and joyful moments must return almost whole.

I remember the house on the hill. Because it was steep, my father carried me to the door then set me down. I was almost five years old, and already I knew and had felt things beyond my years. The house was like one large room inside, and I couldn't take my eyes off my great-uncle, who had lathered up his face and was standing in the light from a small bulb above the corner sink, a straight razor too gleaming in that bulb's poor light.

I heard the happy, loud voices all around me. I watched my grandfather hold a glass of slivovitz high in the air, toasting everything, and then nothing, and drinking the glass in one quick gulp, my grandmother following. I felt the room begin to shrink, and the voices became a soft murmur and, in the only light that matters, I see him slide the razor down his neck as if he were playing the violin. There's a small mirror he leans into, so I can see him twice from where I am, and I don't know why exactly, but it was the happiest I had ever been in my life up to that day, watching him shave that way, wanting it all to be in slow motion so it would last longer.

All memory revolves in fragments, even from the sweet Europeans who were my people of the truest heart, yet singular the image of him, shaving in that small light with such precise perfection I would later know as art. That morning, I watched him finish before he turned to me with his eyes and said something in a language I only barely understood but knew to mean I was free.

Someone on the Train Said *Mecca*

This defeat is so fitting. Ravens are larger than crows is how you know the difference. The Victorians loved the dead. No more flags, no more parades in late summer but

heat like her fingers on my body when I was young and dumber even than I am now. No stars, only holes in an empty sky, kindness natural as honey in the night's shy romance. In some Texas towns, they handcuff you diagonally—right hand over, left hand yanked up, if you haven't learned how to behave. I recommend me unto you, your bridge to nowhere.

For Penelope

Crow Allegro

Essence of crow is my soul, gravity a god bearing down. There is only space enough in my mind to be wrong, fucked. I don't know how to say you died; I left you where you wanted to be that day, my hands bloody from the work. They should not have called you to pull me out. There are other ways to live, although to live without even your joyful madness is not enough.

Start with the split-tongued crow, kept by the woman who lived beside the river, and who taught the crow to speak some words to us boys in wonder, to imagine we understood; end together, behind the bloody curtain of war, from which we could not come back.

Elegy for My Father and the Man in the Moon

My brother Thomas called it that *sad height* and now I know
what he'd meant, here beside my dying father raised up to
the light on his hospice bed, his final bed, and these his final
breaths are precious to me as anything I could hold in my
hand in what used to be the world. The room is dark, the
only noise the human breathlike sound the oxygen machine
makes, as if matching his failing breath. I have said all that I
need to say to him, into his ear, and I hope he did the same.
He wants me in his room this way, he told me with his eyes
today and with his hand that could only barely squeeze my
own to answer yes or no. He is so near his end that the dead
have come into the room to take him home with them where
he belongs, and though he wants us all to let him go, his
warrior's heart keeps fighting at the gates, and I can only
sit and watch him and moisten his dry lips though he no
longer drinks. *Only* I say as if that wasn't enough. The rises
in his chest come less and less. His hands and feet are cold.
I need some air; I go outside in the dark and walk until it's
only the man in the moon and me, there in the indivisible
grief. I thought the man would never lie, or so my father told
me more than once, so tonight I turn to him because there's
no one else for me to ask what words I should say now, as
if goodbye made any sense to those who won't return. The
moon is nearly full and clear as spirits who breathe inside
the frozen sky. The moon won't say a word to me, the man,
he turns away until he's almost gone, no hope for anything
to break the hold that death has on my father's heart and on
his lungs and inside every cell he is. There is no body left for

me or anyone to hold in their useless arms. Only a light that shines inside of him, even as it fades. The moon is bright in the window, the man proud of his work. My father in the hospice bed, his last breaths not a lullaby or a man-in-the-moon song like he would sing to me, a child, making up the words along the way, pointing to the moon that stayed above our poor house and guarded us against the things that try to take your life away before it's time. It's time for me to let him go. I cannot will him back to us but love him still the same.

Part III:

The Name of Beauty on Ngô Quyền Street

At a Car Wash in Little Rock

I used to love to wash my car at night, at a car wash up the street from where I lived with my wife and baby son. At night I sometimes need to slip away. Seldom was there anybody there; that time of night most folks are tucked away and dreaming, so I was startled by a man's voice screaming *Hey asshole,* across the car wash tarmac. I turned around as if it was me he called—it had to be, we were the only ones there—and when I did he yelled again, *No, not you, that other asshole,* but he didn't say it out of disrespect, as it was more a tip of his hat because I knew who I was and had acknowledged it. "Take me to you, imprison me, for I / Except y' enthrall me, never shall be free, / Nor ever chaste except you ravish me," John Donne wrote in his beautiful poem about car washes. Listen, I'm not crazy, I know what he meant: the way you may be overwhelmed by words that come to mean something, only after you've felt their pain.

for Steve Tatum

Lost

I have always had difficulty with directions and have been lost so often over my life that I no longer panic when it happens. You have to be somewhere, I tell myself, when the there isn't there. Once, in the war of many lifetimes ago, at a new landing zone—LZ we called them—I half-walked and half-crawled away from the tent we had pitched that morning to relieve myself of a burden. It wasn't more than fifteen or twenty yards away, but the jungle was thick, and we had only just arrived, so no one was sure about anything. There were no lights or fires allowed at night; not even a smoke, out in the open, so when I finished and pulled my shorts up and grabbed my weapon, I realized that I didn't know what direction I should walk. This is not a problem in the mall, or even in my own neighborhood where I sometimes can't make my way because everything, for a moment or two, looks different. This is a problem, however, on an LZ in northern Việt Nam near Khe Sanh, with a huge contingent of North Vietnamese Regulars moving through the night to begin the Tết Offensive, so I had to be careful about what direction I chose, and there was a minefield nearby as well, and though it was marked off by the EOD guys, it was impossible to see in the dark. I did not panic and instead played out my options. It was early in the morning, three or four; I could try to find my slow way back by trying all directions, or I could wait it out until daylight.

No one would miss me until then. I'd already done my turn at guard and everyone else was asleep. I curled up with an areca palm at my back and tried to get used to seeing in the dark. This feels like an ending to me, although I know it was just a beginning, that night, the beginning of a road through the unimaginable. It's all about the journey, through hemlock and rattle grass; the dog that dropped his prey for its shadow, the chains that fell off, the chasm that was filled, the cross in the sky that means a miracle, the music heard at death, the thoughts discerned.

Tell Them Everything

Tell them everything, they said. Tell them about the sick hands of some evil people or the evil hands of some sick people. Tell them about the one who most betrayed, although a river appears now, so tell them about the river and forget her, whitewater and fat shad wiggling in death at the ends of our gigs, three prongs and waist-deep between rocks where we had to wade our way carefully. More than one of us drowned in that river. We sold the shad to a Russian neighbor who paid ten cents a fish and we were so fucking rich we didn't know what to do. Tell them what you did, they said. Can there be sin without punishment, I asked the Father at catechism on Saturday, my parents too poor for Catholic school, and you had to learn the routine somewhere. I loved the Father, and when I went to war, he wrote to me once a month, but that Saturday morning when I longed only to be on a baseball field, or in the arms of Sister Mary Katherine, fat chance of that, he told me there were questions better left unasked. He didn't say "unanswered," as I had expected, but "unasked." I was disappointed nearly to tears although he never knew that. Afterwards I stayed inside the church alone. I wanted to pray, but nothing would come to my lips, or to my heart, which felt heavy for the first time. I could still hear the stern voice of the Father, warning me about questions my life depended upon me asking. If you have the need to know, there's nothing you can do except open a vein and bleed it out of you. Tell them about the bleeding they said, as if it was easy to pull a hook from a fish's gills. Dome of blue sky is all that we have left between us and one catastrophe or another to wipe it all out, but that's alright with me. Blue sky beyond a green line of old trees bending into the breeze but never letting go, beyond a small house and its many lives that come and go like bats to the last river in the night. Tell them about the night, about the church bells that won't stop ringing, so many dead the rope pulled morning to dusk, no rest for anyone. I wanted to pray under the dome of blue sky, but nothing would come to my lips, and I think it must feel like when a spirit, or something like a spirit, dies inside of you.

For Carolyn F.

Steve

Our cat Steve is such a handsome boy, and sweet, and likes sometimes to play rough, and won't quite tolerate dogs of any kind, and is living proof that animals will be admitted to paradise. Now, insert a dubious neighbor into this picture. She walks her two rowdy dogs past our house. We sometimes say hello but little else. I don't want to say there's something wrong with her; what would that prove? I'll let you judge for yourself once you've heard the whole story. Her clothes are the same, with a babushka; always, the same, over, and over into dizziness if you let yourself focus. I have had indecipherable conversations with her, and although I felt some anger from her, or some hostility, I was also taken in by the beauty of her madness, if I can still use that word, because I don't mean it in a bad way. Besides, I'm a writer, a poet, and her precisely obscure babble was music to me, and to my psyche,

but the myth changes now, and becomes the new myth, and in the new myth the dog walker from down the block corners my wife one day in our garden. She is angry, my wife can tell, and her fists are clenched. She screams at my wife but only about Steve, and how he comes to her house to torment her and her poor dogs to no end, and how we have to keep Steve inside, as if that was possible under the Constitution; animals have rights too, I told her, once she had accosted me. She warned me again about my cat terrorizing her homestead, especially the debonair and unflappable Steve. She said it in a way that made it feel like there were consequences for us, or for Steve, or for young Eddie Gaston, also accused of trespass and dog harassment. I wanted to say something to make her be quiet, and to make her see the wrong in her thinking, but

I took the other way of no confrontation except with my kindness and my compassion, until she walked away. She walked away and then disappeared into a mist that appears when this kind of thing happens, so you don't know then if it happened or not.

For Jean

Glory

When the rain came, the sky was shuttered with gray clouds turning almost to black. Some people thought it was the end of days, the old flood story, but instead of an ark, they built houses on stilts on cliffs near the ocean whose views are so beautiful, one or two must fall off the face of the earth every year as sacrifice, into the abyss that is the growing ocean. That's prestige real estate; the kind you must be able to afford to lose or you have no business joining the neighborhood. And you don't have to tell me twice that I don't belong there. For a long time, I thought the two forks were in case you dropped one. I belong among words as if words never betray, and the smell of fish has arrived as the rain ends, wind from the north, then over our great lake, bringing the smell of fish all the way to this small room, a kind of glory, you could say.

Summer Flash 2017

You are in the abandoned meadow you always find your way to, no matter what other kinds of spinning goes on in your brain. No, listen. I want to try to explain this.

You're driving your car home on a route you know for mostly your whole life, through farms and then a little city traffic, and you're calm in that after-work way, looking forward to seeing your family, and kicking back; you couldn't be any further away from the war, the way that space doesn't change and only expands, but a sharp and loud noise from a truck, like metal splintering and letting go, sends you right back to a convoy on Highway #1 headed north to Khe Sanh and hammered by everything imaginable all along the way. I have to be careful here. It's not a cartoon, or a movie, but more a way of being able to watch your life spin out of control right in front of you, but I didn't wreck the car, and I kept driving right through the time it took for an RPG to blow a deuce-and-a-half ahead of ours in the convoy nearly in half. This shouldn't happen to anyone, would be my argument.

For Francis

Dear, the invisible bees in their seagrass meadow glassing the great sun in New Jerusalem, painted with bells to kiss her downfall on the Mount Onion deaf, the opium poppy, the bees that turned to glass like a comet over Broadway, a black body that had to steal a small light from inside of her body, until there was nothing left to hold. Think about it like that, motherfucker, if you can. Think about how you took and how you keep on taking. Forgiveness is overrated, especially when it comes to the so-called self; some people give up their right to be forgiven. It's not a law exactly, but something we understand naturally, like she of the jeweled road, like the smoking mirror, and the Lord of the close vicinity.

Fire Fish

Once a week I have the privilege to teach a handful of inner-city kids at risk how to write. We write poems together in class and then read them out loud. I am, and I am not, amazed at how good the writing is, how sweet and how needful to be released into the air, and I'm a selfish man because I keep most of my joy to myself, and don't tell them how their poems bring alive for me the neighborhood of my childhood. When I said I was teaching them, I wasn't saying it right. They are teaching me with every syllable they pull out of themselves like a fine thread barely visible in the light. Our worlds are not so different, I want them to know; they want me to know how different they are.

For Joan Perch

Liquor Was Involved

I was on my way to the rat lab one lonely Sunday evening in my undergraduate days where I went to school with very smart people who had had advantages. I had had a war. That night, I had to do some tasks in the Skinner box, which I hated for how it punished my rat whom I had come to love over our long semester together; he could complete five continuous tasks, even after he'd become dehydrated, or after I'd starved him for a few days, but the science made less and less sense to me as I went on, and I already knew by then that I could no longer experiment on animals, so when she called to me from across the courtyard I was glad to hear her voice out there in the cold. We met halfway. In some light that came through the frozen oaks she looked so beautiful I could only smile and laugh. She laughed too and said we should get a drink to warm up. I told her I was heading to the lab, that I had to force my poor, dehydrated and starving rat whom I refused to name to complete several annoying tasks, so I could pass the course and the rat could eat and drink. She laughed again and said she'd come to help me, so we could finish fast and then go for that drink. I liked to be alone with my work, especially when it involved abusing animals, but she had a way about her that you could not say no to. In the lab I knew immediately that she knew what she was doing. For most folks it was an eerie place at night, the small room full of small cages full of white rats mostly, and some pigeons and rabbits as well to whom neurological damage had already been done, but she made herself at home looking around, and once I'd flipped the light on, she asked me where he was. I walked to the cage and met her there. I gave her a glove and told her to reach inside and bring the rat out. Not surprisingly, he bit her finger a little and when she dropped him, and I picked him up, he bit my finger as well, but he'd done that before and I knew to hold on until he finally calmed down. I stroked his head with my bare finger now and so did she and she purred with the rat against her cheek and then dropped it into the box. Mostly he wanted water, and without any prompts or words of encouragement, he immediately began to go through the routine that he and I had learned together through classical conditioning, so that in the end, it was difficult to tell the teacher from the student. We finished my assignment quickly and the work looked good. She helped me write some notes that were required, explaining exactly how the rat had behaved and then we were on our way into the cold again.

Have you ever felt a beautiful woman take your hand in the cold and hold it close to her face? I breathed deeply and wondered, truly wondered to myself, if I was in heaven, or paradise, to be in the care of someone who wanted only to protect me from myself. Her beauty was of the kind that made it difficult for me to breathe. She drank with me, so I wouldn't drink alone. We sat on the same side of the booth and listened to Chuck Berry on the juke box. I don't remember now why I thought that everything was coming down to that moment, but I did, and I even felt the weight of the sky coming down and the power of the earth pushing up, and I could hear a low rumbling that sounded like thunder only longer and deadlier. She picked my head up off the table with both her hands. It's time to go, she said, and helped me stand and zipped my coat. I had thought I couldn't walk anywhere, but I did, on her arm, through a cold snowy night so tender you could reach out and touch it. I didn't know where I was or where I was going anymore. She stood me against the brick front of her place, and I heard her keys jingle and then the lock snap open. Inside I found a couch or bed and let myself go there. I felt I needed to hide from someone who was coming for me through the snow. I tried to explain this, but she put her finger to my lips and put a cool washcloth across my forehead and told me she knew that I would be alright.

In the rat lab the rats were running through their routines in their minds. They don't dream of an empty Skinner box, but of a wild grassy field cut through by a cool stream. I passed out and had no dreams I could remember, which was satisfactory in those post-war days, and when I woke, I saw her face before I saw anything else. Some things cannot be explained with math or logic. Some things only make sense in your heart. The way someone's care can be a river that holds you up, and then sends you on your way to be free.

for D.

Epistle to God

"Dear God," I began my letter when I was seven years old. I could read and write thanks to my father who never graduated from high school but who taught me how to live in the world like a man, like how to read a box score, and score a game by myself, and how to throw a punch. That's something. But I was writing to God to save myself from sins I thought so horrible, God would put an end to my miserable life. I didn't worry about the delivery of my letter to God and put my stupid faith in the mailbox on the corner where I'd once frozen my lips to the side, hiding from a police car in the winter night. There was nothing left but chances by then. The arcade was closing down, its lights blinking off, one by one. Better not to ask why things happen, a waste among some wider wastes; nothing left except what's left.

Our Recent Way

As the hurricane "weakened" to a fucking tropical storm,
the stock market rose. You could feel it in the air as a kind
of pressure, until it felt like surely something would burst
open and spew green money. All you can hope for is a favorite
song to come over the radio, or unexpectedly, for the hinge of
the Way, where this and that no longer find their opposites,
to open. No one, Chuang Tzu wrote, has lived longer than
a dead child.

Some Ohio Cows

I don't remember how I ended up walking through pitch-black countryside, Amish country, so only a dim lamp here and there, scattered like secrets. I had talked myself out of being afraid and I was walking in what I fully believed was the right direction, the lake always north, my reference point. I may have said a prayer to myself or sung a song. I knew I had some ways to go, miles even, and through the dark Ohio countryside, alone. Just like now, I didn't know how I had come to be there, or why, or even where I was exactly. This was before the war, but I had already learned some things,

so I kept my head up and marched down the road with the moon and oh, all at once the field was lit with the floating white faces of cows, so I jumped in the moment it took for my brain to recognize what I was seeing, and when I saw, I laughed out loud with joy and with the kind of relief that comes when you learn you will survive. Later,

in Quảng Tri Province, as I huddled in a bunker with four or five others trying to stay alive under a rocket attack, I remembered how afraid I had been that night when I first saw the cows' white faces floating there like something I didn't want to know about, and how good the whole thing felt when I realized they were only cows. It's confusing, I know. The moments get slammed together that way, so I don't know what to do.

The Name of Beauty on Ngô Quyển Street

I'm addicted to beauty. I'm dying of beauty on Ngô Quyển Street in the hotel the French built in another century of blood and people hung in doorways all the way to hell. I'm trapped inside of beauty for the way things are what they are and then are not and then are what they truly are, the lesson not difficult. Beauty is difficult,

when you breathe it in like oil of lilac, oil of meadowsweet, as if you could repair the harmed soul of anyone, never mind your own. Even the executioner has his charming moments. I am only safe inside of words.

Fa-Hien's Magic Cow
Four Hundred Years Before Christ

The sage Vashishtha kept a magical cow. You cannot imagine what this cow could do. The King wanted the cow because he was the King and could make claim to all things in his kingdom, but the story goes that the Chinese protected the sage Vashishtha and kept the King from possessing the magical cow and thus found a kind of balance in all things. We know this from pictures, not words. The nomads had no texts, no books on silk for the Han. What is the dream of the red mansion? Who is the Monkey King? The delusion in despair is the same as that in hope.

Lost in Beijing

I want to sail away on the stone boat of *No Name Lake* with you, away from the noise of the city beating like a heart. I want to disappear into the nothing, clear as the lakes inside of stars.

Then there is the kind of lesson the cold teaches you; the gas in the flat not yet turned on, so I head outside into sunlight on the street on my first day and feel warmer but am instantly lost though I didn't panic knowing all along that I had to be somewhere, no matter what, and along the way somehow I wanted to hold the 9th-century inlaid porcelain vase, but it was not allowed, the expert told me. He held it in his white-gloved hands as if it was alive because it was, to him, and it took him back to an ancient time, and an ancient people whom he could feel silently talking inside of him.

Some kind strangers finally found my way for me, and even guided me to my sixth-floor walk-up's ground floor entrance, among buildings indistinguishable from one another to me. I was glad to be back in the flat, however cold it felt. I put on extra clothes and when I still shivered in the middle of the day, I wrapped myself in a quilt that brought beads of sweat to my forehead and eventually through my shirt, but I loved the warmth. It was a promise someone keeps after a long time of betrayals and coldness of the heart. I wasn't sure where I was, but I felt safe, wrapped up in two quilts on a flat reed bed in a small room with a window that looked far down into the empty courtyard of all my desire.

Milkweed Pods

The first thing I saw when I came back and found Ohio again were some milkweed pods open in the first frost, their silk filaments needful of any wind at all to ride on. The maple leaves are gone in early November, some oak trees keep their leaves until the end of winter in Ohio; the Chinese elm is almost bare, and you can feel how much light comes in again, this time of year. The way the light can flatten the long shadows of trees out across the neighborhood lawns like solemn monuments to the not-quite-dead, the not quite living, like my dream of the red mansion, trapped in Ohio. But even these black monuments fade as the sun fades until there is only a filament of light between what you can bear and what you can't, because this is where you have arrived, and this is who you are, if you are anything at all, some shape beauty moves, a clear conceiving down and out that surrounds you.

For J.W. in memoriam

Elegy for One Soul

I was thinking about someone's death this morning, while athletes on the news were kneeling all over America to the sound of our national anthem. My friend who died used to say: *No justice no peace*, and in his end, there was very little peace, but if you call dying justice, well, he got his.

They are kneeling because of what is wrong with our country, and my friend who died fought the same battle for fifty years of his life but was never on the television. Sometimes the darker clouds come in and hang so low there's nothing you can do but hunker down and wait for them to pass. Sometimes your own thoughts can carry you into the swamp of debris that is memory. *What can the river do to help* is what I keep thinking, but I may have been drowning when this was going on. I may have been raped by adults under a wool blanket in a cold apartment. I may have been trapped in a bunker for three days while the LZ exploded around us, but that shouldn't keep me from telling it all, as if I could dip into the great lake of All and find something there that made sense, that made us all feel a little better.

Earring

I didn't know then or would not allow myself to know that she was trying to find a way to say goodbye to me. Outside in the cold December snow one night, we had a stupid argument about something stupid, and let it go past certain boundaries, I think, of hurt. I didn't know what the problem was. I tried to talk to her, but then during all of that, she lost an earring in the deep snow when she slammed her head into one of the historic elms where she had run into the dark to get away from me, or from her own longing. For a long time, I couldn't find her, not until she came back, crying and begging me to help her find the earring. Her sister had given it to her many years before, she said, but I wasn't sure why someone would cry so hard over a lost earring. I was still a boy, though I'd seen the war and some hard things, so I promised her I'd find her earring. She is cold and shaking. I'm on my hands and knees in the dark among huge elm trees. I can feel the rhythm of the night beat and pulse like a heart. I make a grid and then feel my way with gloveless hands through the snow as if I were feeling for the edge of a landmine trigger.

The snow continues to fall on me, and on the elm trees already heavy, and on the whole landscape of our dreams, so everything is white again, transformed into mute monuments of itself. My knees soak through and begin to freeze. My fingers I can no longer feel, but still, out of love I stay out there, looking for the tiny spray of gold in the tons of snow, as if finding it would somehow ensure her love for me, but then the wind blows hard for a fool, and in that chill I get a good look at myself, on my hands and knees, searching for a tiny gold earring in the snow, and there is joy inside

of my tears when I find the earring, buried in snow, among
the elm trees that you could hide behind, in ambush.

For Alison

Camp Evans Blues

Listen—three NVA soldiers that we had as POWs at our basecamp thirty-five clicks north of Huế City escaped one day in the middle of the afternoon. With practically everyone else I was sent out with my weapon to find them before dark. It wasn't a big deal at the time, more a distraction from the usual boredom. We worked in teams of two and looked everywhere on the base camp where someone could hide, but they weren't around. By then the sun was already on the horizon so you could see the hills light up like temples in the green. Ready to head back to command, I saw a man squatting in that Vietnamese way, as if he was trying to blend in with the flat landscape, and he nearly did, but as we walked towards him, our weapons locked and loaded, I could make out his features and the frightened look on his face. I wondered why he had escaped his cage, what he expected us to do. He put his hands in the air. He wore a simple shirt and shorts and carried nothing with him. We were at the far end of the base camp, near the perimeter. Only three of us out there, and for reasons I don't fully understand, the idea that not all of us would make it back home was the feeling I had about the whole enterprise. We guided and half-dragged him to command and to the holding area, and at the first opportunity, I learned later, he ran away again into what had become night. Artillery was already booming nearby, the sharp, concussive blasts pulling the skin from our bones for that instant of what—worry? Forgiveness? Hope?

In Memory of Captain Casey

Ohio Pastoral

What's left of the bent-up corn is dusted with snow. Through the arctic Ohio air, crows dive for what's left before an even harder winter sets in, all the muskrat ponds I haunted now frozen over or disappeared in memory. Yet there is always the question of winter and the new year, and what it is that hides from me in the folded tabletops of snow, drifting so high sometimes we were lost for days yet never missed. Someday, I'll tell you something funny, and something terrible. The snow at night knows all of it, but it won't say.

Elegy for Zora Grasa

Midnight and I'm up watching the storm bury us all under the testimony of snow, and I think about my mother, buried now two days already in her death, and in the folds of cold earth. I don't want her back; that's not what I'm asking. I only want her to be warm enough on the journey.

The snow is even dizzying in the sharp gusts of wind and in the street light's arc, and there is something that keeps coming to me, that image, that precise feeling of loss. I would trade the treasures of the world to be in your arms, your fingers on my forehead, singing me the song of the stone boats, and the spirits who ride them home. . .

Us Children

The moon could tell the truth about the deep snow and what waits for us there. It's not a plan exactly but has to do with how it's possible to move from one world into another. The skeleton winter trees understand this. They bare themselves to whatever comes, and though they shudder, they never cry out, and they can stand against almost anything.

You might be in the middle of a fallback where you can't keep track of where you are, or whose clouds want to stand sideways in the mirror where it's not, dear, yourself; you see?

Are those cries I hear coming from an ocean of hurt I'm certain is just across town, behind the curtain where the bad stuff unfolds? Stay with me; I'm trying to say something straight, but it's so cold here, and I don't want a rendezvous with anyone, thank you, especially in the tunnels of snow, where I am safe like you, as the faithless sky watches over us.

Cognitive Blue

I've been trying to strip something away so that I could see the jungle more clearly. You get it? It's not me who wants this really, but my doctor, and I want to please her. I want her to never release my best madness to anyone, and she won't. In the corner of her office on the floor, I let myself travel back to some moments so shrouded in terror I lose my way when they cross my mind like explosive white shrieks. I lose my way and have wrecked my car, forgetting I was driving and the one responsible.

In the way of seeing clearly is some smoke, and many explosions. In the way are some unidentifiable screams that won't stop shuddering through the razor grass. Screaming in any language sounds the same. If it's true what they say about the circle, then this will all be over soon, but only to start again. This is not a movie in my head, not a rationalization of any kind, not a textbook fear, but a coronary way of being somehow always on the verge of falling off the edge of something not quite visible through the mist. I want you to write this all down please, doctor, because I'm afraid that I won't remember. I feel like the deal between us obligates you to tend that gate we pass through.

Lunch at the Wade Park VA Cafeteria, Early Twenty-First Century

Some people still haven't learned how to behave and so must be dragged away, handcuffed, and loudly professing the legitimacy of their new world philosophy. Otherwise, it's mostly quiet, so I like to eavesdrop on the conversations of my fellow veterans. It's not the context that I'm after, see, or even the story, but just a word or two, here and there, a fragment, smuggled from someone else's life without their knowledge. *Harvest was the hell this year,* the man with the backwards baseball hat says. *But if you die,* someone declares across the room, *you're finally fucking free.* And then a doctor, her white coat stained with blood, says *I've seen people wear down that way,* her hands spread before her, as if she was trying to illustrate the suffering. Someone shakes their head "yes," and someone else shakes it "no." Some deals are settled upon by all parties.

Winter and the New Year

Snow as heavy all across the northern parts of the state as wide as the satellite can see, and I don't want to write or talk about anything except the pain of cold the homeless feel on nights like this. That penetrating cold that won't let you be warm all night long, so you shudder, if you're lucky, and you don't fucking freeze to death. This happens, brothers and sisters, and I know the bare winter trees out there in the dubious night mean something, empty branches rattling like an empty cupboard. There is no algorithm for that kind of suffering, no matter what you say, only a long chain of not having, strung out through history as far back as we may travel. Winter says, this is the way of things, and then it covers everything in a ghostly white that mutes the sound of the earth beating but allows passage for all beings.

Cow Moves in with Bison Herd, Warsaw, Poland, 2018

She would not be made an offering of any kind, and so this solitary cow escaped her pen and joined a herd of protected and endangered bison, roaming the countryside in all their big-headed glory. She is the talk of Wasilkowo, says Rafal Kowalczyk, a bison expert who managed to photograph this unusual sight, and who says this relationship is dangerous to both sides. A reddish-brown cow that must look like a child to the bison whose heads are nearly the size of her body, would not survive the birth of her hybrid calf because of the unforgiving differences in size. On the other side is the complex contamination of a gene pool of already endangered animals who roam the countryside freely now. She has been faithful to the bison, and they gather sometimes around her. She is finding enough to eat. The snow is falling all over eastern Poland. She has defied the slaughterhouse for now, and the only question is will she follow them into the forest when winter ends.

Clinical Notes Number Ninety-One

I don't know who is driving this car, but it ain't me, was the last thought in my head before the car left the roadway and headed over a ditch, into a field of broken corn, then between two huge elms that shrugged their shoulders as I laid on the brakes and finally slid to a stop near someone's front porch. You think you know what a flashback is, but you don't, because of the disguises they come in, because of the way their mere appearance is enough to alter the laws of physics in your mind momentarily. I want to tell you about this, but it's so difficult to say the words in such a way as to bring the moment to your good table, so you could sit down with me, but the tired wallpaper tells me to shut up, and the weary door that sags tells me to let whoever wants to, come in. I want to say more, but I'm afraid now of speaking all my impulses out of existence. You can get the drift of that if you've ever been under fire, can't you? Then there's the flashing-forward part no one ever talks about. A jolt so quick and hard back into the world, you feel as if your spine may snap in two. First, you're there, if only for a second long enough to wreck your mind, and then you're back, so to speak.

When Steve Pulled Through

we had already begun our mourning for him, and in our minds, we were already looking for a kitten replacement from the rescue house. He had all the symptoms of a dying cat, and in his eyes with which he never hesitated to meet mine, he looked like he was ready to let go and finally enter the stream of space that blasts past us not like a train exactly, but close. I saw something in his eyes, but it turns out not to have been death or dying, just some seriousness of which he wanted us to take note, and then to care for him. When you have a friend like that, who doesn't speak the language, and who may be in some distress with no way to tell you, you have to be especially on guard. Being on guard means slowing the world down and paying attention to things right down to their atoms, spinning in their beautiful eccentricity all around your head like so many moons in orbit around a dying planet. Please, don't even get close to me now, the spirit says.

No Irritable Reaching

The rooftops are all covered in frozen snow. Nothing moves in the last light except the bare branches that rattle an ancient song about loss and separation, about the dreams some people believe in, right up to the last moment. I wonder what dream kept him alive for his short life. He was so young, yet he said all that needs to be said about joy, and about what death means—that waking dream that isn't sleep because the music's fled.

The Still Unravished Bryn of Quietude

I knew a woman once named Bryn who lived in a trailer, although it wasn't in a park, but in the city, near the steel mill behind some abandoned buildings. The rent was cheap, and it came that she invited me to stay there with her awhile. We were poor and didn't have a car or much else except what the G.I. Bill could buy in nineteen seventy something, and with her tips from the rowdy bar where she said she'd found her peace. I was in college. It was just after the war. I think she was lonely like me, especially at night, when she came home late from the bar where she waitressed until two or three. I would sleep late and then get up and walk home with her the five or six blocks through nothing good, night after night, and when we arrived, she would empty her apron of her tips from the long day, with which also comes humiliation, and she would give the money to me as if she was presenting me with a sword, or with some kind of award, and she would smile when I refused and tried to push the money back. Some people have the kind of smile that can look back through thousands of years so that when their light falls on you, you can feel them through your whole body like the shiver that joy is. I needed the light of that smile, and the feel of her body against mine at night when she fell asleep in my arms. Like her, I needed the unnameable force that love is, and we had found something like that one night, dancing drunk in a drunken bar, until we danced all the way to her trailer, and spent more than a few nights there in her bed, listening to the A.M. radio and sometimes singing along. This is what a life can be. But later, I would get busy at school, stay in the dorm, and not see her for a while, a week or so, and once, one of her friends called, frightened, and told me that Bryn needed me. A pal drove me there and dropped me off. I thought she'd be at work, but I liked to listen to the A.M. radio in the trailer, and to wait for Motown to come on, and for her to come home, but when I got there, I found several people milling around the small front porch of the trailer, whose door was open even in the cold, and more people out in the street nearby. I walked through the open door and saw her lying there, on the couch that someone had covered with starched, white sheets. She was pale and her face was swollen and bloody. She was being tended to by local nurses the neighbors had called after she made her way home from where she'd been taken by three strange men in a car. They had robbed her on her way home from work. They tore off her apron full of tip money. It was the middle of winter, in Ohio. They made her take her clothes off in the car and beat her with a pistol when she was too slow, then they dumped her in a snowy field near the pipe mill. Naked, she made her way home through the still-dark morning and the unbearable cold, alone, and once outside her own door, she began to scream, and didn't stop, the neighbors said, until police arrived. You can be alive after something like that; you can work and dance and sing and maybe even fall in love after something like that, but it would never be okay. I saw her only once more, a few years later at a flea market in the country where she let me hold her hand while we talked, but she never let her eyes find my eyes again, although I wanted her to see how I had taken on the grief, and that if only I had been there for her, it never would have happened. But when she pulled her hand away, it was as if a curtain came down between us, and I knew it was the end of something that had haunted me, that had teased me out of thought more than a few times, like a nightmare whose ending you can't remember, and so have to keep having again and again. I don't care what you say about love; one heart is always lonely for another heart, until it finds the one that soothes the beating, that erases the sound of bullets, exploding all around you.

Clinical Notes Number Ninety-Two

You're waiting for the spring to find its way, though winter wants to stay with us awhile. It clings with icy fingers to our hearts, the cold that you can feel so deep inside you think you'll never know the warm again. You're waiting for the angle of the sun to change enough to let you breathe a little easier, the sky an invitation to a blue as endless as the suffering of souls that you may hear, their hollow voices carried on the wind at night that speaks a tongue that only those who open their minds can understand. You understand?

I'm saying this so I can stay alive, because I'm only safe inside the words, the song of words that flows through all my veins, the blood I need to stay with you awhile. The only other choice I have, to let the strands of light that hold me here release me from the weight of seeing the death I carry with me like a ruck; release me from the burdens that only nights with the faint smell of sulfur understand. The problem is I don't know what I want; if I let go, there's nothing left of me except the boy I was before the sky fell down.

I see him sometimes walking with a gun through brilliant sun and emerald green, the danger only feet away. I see him sometimes hiding in a hole as dark as blood while rockets sail in like freight trains through his brain. You understand? This circle never ends; there's always this dark hit parade of favorite moments blasted out of time by fear that you can taste and feel right through your gut. It's time to go. I've said too much.

Standing Before the Arch of Triumph in Bucharest, I Think of Lorain, Ohio and of Quảng Trị Province, Việt Nam

I took a rest in Bucharest to try and pray some things away and pray some things to stay. Red pepper. Yellow pepper. Cheese and black bread dipped in coal black coffee. Why are there no stars is a question I won't ask out loud. I lose things, but then I find them again because it's all still here you know, like in the highlands, yeah, a cemetery we had hoped would keep us safe from shelling or ambush—the ancestor worship protecting us—fat chance of that, or near the roundhouse where I'd wandered into trouble as a boy. Someone held my head there in their hands, and still I knew nothing about the brutally simple facts, and you think I would have, given all the falling down stairs I had to navigate. I don't want to start lying to you after everything we've been through, but there was a dark woman with darker eyes from Moldova who told me a thing or two in private, and taught me a thing or two, her mind a wild star tumbling through an ancient history, although it is difficult to translate one way of thinking into another. It doesn't matter what we want, and the end of feeling is worse than death whether you're up marching around or not. But you must admire how in Bucharest they slow their meals down so they become a sweet sharing of things said and unsaid, a communion of common bread, the way they did in South Lorain at the crowded tables of my immigrant family, loud curses and loud prayers, my Serbo-Croat grandfather holding forth, a philosopher in work clothes, at what I thought as a child would be the last meal of our lives.

Sutra

I am brother of the gutted cardinal the cats brought home and left like a bloody gift on the stoop for us to find in the morning. I am brother of the cats who kill as guiltlessly as a god, and I am brother of the mud the god rises from to stand there like a tree we don't know we should care for. I am brother of the trauma like a river through my brain, and never subsides; see? I am brother of the crow who speaks to me, but I am not free like the crow to choose the way the world appears, and I don't know what I'm asking for here, except a hand to reach back through those years and bring me home because I am brother of three bad days and three bad nights when they blew us up. I am brother of the dizzying lift ship I saw smash down so hard into the wire that it burst into flames and then disappeared, those who had come to get us out, souls I imagined who drifted up from the flames and smoke of the wreckage all the way to hell. Just when you think there are answers, another scream shudders down the dark hallway in the night. I am brother of the night that holds us forth like pure finders of our own mortal shrines. Nothing should be left to chance.

Drawing I

I wanted to draw a picture of the landscape I often visit without my permission, but whatever the pencil does is not right. The pencil in my hand is not right, so the trees look instead like gallows, and the birds like daggers flying, and the mountain I tried to sketch becomes a burden I must carry on my back like a rucksack through the jungle. You know? All I fucking wanted to do was draw a picture of the landscape that included trees of several engaging varieties, not many birds, I admit, some mountains in the distance that called me, and some wild animals that would emerge in darkness from the brush into the mowed lawn of my mountain home, but everything I drew looked like death somehow, or like dying, and no matter how I held the pencil, or in which direction I dragged it, it all had the same flat countenance of death.

I don't think this means anything though, because right at this moment I'm watching the pink and white azaleas blossom into such beauty that I feel like I will never die. And although it's only a feeling, a glimpse of something and then gone, it's all the honey hole of joy that I need at this moment. May I speak to you as if you were reading this?

Bad Day

The air comes cold from rivers before dawn. The convoy had to cross at night: one man perched on each hood, pointing left or right, guiding the drivers around rocks and holes, no lights allowed. I watched one deuce-and-a-half float off in the current when they'd veered off and hit a hole; the occupants scrambled to get out like crabs before I lost them in the swirling dark. Before dawn, the air comes cold from rivers. I sat on the hood and tried to see our way across the biggest rocks looming up from the bottom like bodies of the dead in our wake. Do you believe me when I tell you that I wanted that river whose name I don't remember to churn up and take me away to the bottom? Well I did. I thought it was the only thing that would save me, and I don't know what saved me from more than a few cheap deaths, but before dawn, from rivers, the air comes cold and makes me lonesome for just one sane minute. We were on the verge, you could say. We'd been on the road for days and shelled every night. We had to cross the river in our trucks at night. We were watched from trees by men who would later murder us. There were no lights allowed so I sat on the hood and pointed our way through the darkness that swept over me like someone's arms trying to hold me back from my sacrifice, and when we made it across, we could see the other trucks again, gathering like at a carnival or fair. We lost one truck, I heard the sergeant say, and one boy too who drowned inside his truck. We waited there in the dark for his body; the truck had washed ashore downstream, not far. Nothing would be said about it, ever. I didn't know his name, though I'd seen him try to struggle free as his truck was swept away in the current, and I didn't even think of what to do.

Evening Prayer

Some pain your body always knows no matter how long it's been. Pain of rockets and mortars exploding all around you, so that it takes only a car backfire or something heavy, dropped onto the floor behind your back, to set the whole landscape off in your mind where it's etched in electro-chemical perfection.

My dead friends I still love something of, although not the mass, or the pulse of blood through the neck, and more a way of feeling them move through me in their jungle fatigues and with their boyish, their sometimes baby, faces. Just a glimpse though, then they're gone.

Thăng Long

Substantial moonlight was all that was required, and a thousand-year-old city waking up like a dragon, and some đàn bầu strains near the lake where the great tortoise lives and keeps his myth alive. He knew what to do with a sword, or so the story goes. I knew what to do with your hand in my hand like a lily, resting in the shallows under shade, because there are certain moments you should not allow to leak through the sky full of seams and passageways, full of easy ways out. I don't want an easy way. I am no longer fearful of the mist, as I once was. I can wake up now on a riverbank and not worry who is there to kill me. In fear and in love we seek a syncopated heartbeat to keep ourselves from spinning off the world, and this is neither a good nor a bad thing, only a way to count out, no matter what, the heartbeats you have left, Buddhas everywhere you look, their hands folded in prayer, holding up what we imagine is the sky. We don't want or need a horizon like we thought all this time; that's not the way things work. The way things work is like this: you don't have a job and so not enough money to marry your sweetheart, and you can only be alone with her by the lake, at night, sharing a bench under the Buddha moon, holding hands, and talking in the hushed tones of betrayal, of joy.

On the Road to Bổ Đà Pagoda

The temple where we're all headed on this Hà Nội office excursion is four hundred years old and to pray there to the teachers, and to the Buddha, is to pray through the mist of our world into another. At nine a.m. we cross the Red River on the Vĩnh Tuy Bridge. The driver's name is Thiên. He tells me in Vietnamese, before he says anything else, that he loves to wear American military clothes. He's proud of his Air Force Academy ring, he says, and of the U.S. Army fatigues he has on, and the Marine Corps duty cap. Without missing a gear in the five-speed van, he opens his large phone to show me some photographs. At first, I don't understand. They are group pictures of men and women of different ages dressed in American military garb of a wide variety. I ask him in Vietnamese if those people are the Army and he says yes, happily. He points to the picture and says the word Army in Vietnamese several times. He tells me that his father had been a policeman, a chief of police in Hà Nội, and shows me a photograph of him in his uniform. He drives but talks at the same time, so we get lost along the way and end up stuck in traffic on a street too small for our van to turn around in. Everyone in the vicinity offers instructions to the driver who ignores them all and does what he does for a living with the cool expertise of another kind of master. And there is no tension, or frustration, no anger, only laughter at our fate. Why are they so different than us. At the pagoda we pray in pairs and sometimes alone. The peace and grace, I feel in my heart and in my mind. On the way home we stop at a roadside restaurant to eat the fat of the pig, boiled with garlic and fish sauce, and to drink rice whiskey some people make on their own, full of the Buddha's love.

On Thiền Quang Lake, Nguyễn Du, Hà Nội, Spring 2019

The fishing's bad in any language, the weather cool, the pressure falling. Because I'm sometimes lonely here, I walk around this lake in the morning and then again at night so that by now some faces are familiar to me, and mine to them. I've known this neighborhood for years; the people seldom change. The barber moved from his corner but remains nearby. Listen, I walk around this small lake in Hà Nội in the morning and at night. Black swans swim here but mostly they hide in the rushes. White swans swim sometimes beside them, sometimes not. Old men play a kind of Chinese chess, eight characters times infinity and you must think quickly. One man tried to teach me how to play. Don't look, he said and turned my gaze away from the board. Now, play, he said. One man snags with a treble hook he throws nearly across the lake, then drops the small silver fish onto the concrete bank where they slowly die. An older man watches his bobber move a few feet offshore. A woman courts a small business there, a thermos or two of tea, a few cigarettes, some chickens caged nearby for later in the day; for the fishermen, who don't want to go home.

Living in a City Without Guns

The votive paper burns for the recent dead, lighting up this Hà Nội street corner as the sun goes down. It gets dark early here in spring, and a light mist of rain called *mưa xuân* hangs like a lace curtain over everything. I don't know much about death, although I have seen more than my share. I'm certain of that. I don't know much about longing either, although I had believed it was longing that kept me unfulfilled. The lily pad is never unfulfilled, nor is the wren whose small song you can hear even deep in the forest. Yet these are all only thoughts, aren't they? Things that bounce around through space like tiny satellites for the grief-stricken souls who can never go home.

What a frightful place that we inhabit; what a place to raise your kids. More guns than people, and little to hold them back.

Hot Waters

Do you think the lushness of the green grass isn't enough to make me be alive, or the spring leaves splintering through the branches like tiny explosions of light? It's too wet to mow, so the grass has taken over all across the neighborhood. In May not all the birds are back; I'm waiting for a few who return every year and help me mark the time, the ones who survive the wicked cats. Do you think the stone-cold color of the sky means more than it says? It's wrong to see omens where there are no omens but even worse to miss them when they're there. Like turning down a wrong avenue that leads to a dead end that leads to a pier on the dark lake where the ore boats slink their way. Do you think there's a reason for this loneliness beyond the vultureless sky enough to make you want to stick around? The pier is empty for a change, so we have our choice of spots. This early in the morning, bodies sometimes float past. The huge machine that turns the railway cars upside down to dump the coal starts up before the sun is up, its rhythmic slamming of metal, a beat that you can feel after a while. I took my love down there.

for Richard Olijar

Waiting for the Cardinals

I watched for them all morning until they finally came, she more beautiful than her red husband, more precise in her choice of hollow grass she'll weave into the nest. It's May, and I watch them do everything together, safe for the moment from the mortal dangers of cats we love like our children who have gone away now, the way everything goes away. Sometimes they winter over. Somehow, one of the pair manages to survive because they come back every year, the same treeline where they build a nest and flash across my field of vision. I know that I am satisfied.

What the Teacher Said

Why are you looking at me, the woman in the airport business-class lounge said to someone that I didn't know was me until she said it again, leaning towards me and looking directly into my eyes. I said what was on my tongue; that I had looked at her because she was beautiful, in that rare way that beauty has to uplift you, but that I hadn't meant to stare. I had remembered the lesson. Embrace beauty, the teacher said, let it wash over you, let the wildflowers drowning the landscape wash over you, let the white-capped river of voices wash over you, and then let it go, but I can find no way to tell her this, so I turn away. I show her my back to comfort her. Notre Dame is burning on the television. There's nothing left to do but take the beauty in, and then let it wash over you.

The Price of Roses in Hà Nội

I bought some roses on Đỗ Hành Street in the early morning bustle and my friend said I paid too much and scolded the seller who had walked in from the countryside. She smiled and tucked away the money I had given her. Once I explained to my friend how each rose was just now opening its buds, so that during the next day or so new flowers would continually blossom, he relented a little, but still argued that I had paid too much, and to let him do it the next time.

I didn't care about the cost although I know I should have. I only wanted some new roses for the people who help take care of me. I wanted them to be able to watch the roses blossom from day to day, right into their lives. The price of roses in Hà Nội depends upon where they come from, where you buy them, and at what stage of your life, and their lives, they are suspended.

Driving to Làng Chùa

On the anniversary of his mother's death, I drive with my friend to his village where his family goes back eight generations, although what we will do there, I'm not certain. I know the village, Làng Chùa—Pagoda Village—and have slept there in old rooms in the perfect dark and celebrated Tết, house to house one chilly winter, but I've never come here to honor the dead. I was in my room, trying not to feel the emptiness I had been practicing to feel when my friend called, asking me to join him. In the village of Làng Chùa they celebrate the dead in vivid memory, and after delivering to the altar a bounty of food and gifts, they turn to their own feast of simple country food. The moment shimmers now in my mind and I want to keep it there, the food, the home-made whiskey, the laughter and feel of family reaching back so far into the darkness until there's only light. Tonight, alone, I hear only a single dog speak for the night. Do you hear it? Never mind. It's only words.

For Nguyễn Quang Thiều

Meditation on Yết Kiêu Street, Hà Nội, About Ohio

I saw a crippled man today selling sundries on the street where I live, although this is about Ohio and the man who didn't speak and who could barely walk and so frightened us as children as he made his way around the neighborhood, dragging one leg that seemed dead to me, mumbling, and drooling when he passed us on the street, a grimace always on his face. We wouldn't get close although some of us called him names and some of us copied his terrible limp and followed him down the street, mocking him. We didn't know his name, or where he lived until one day a rough kid from my block got smacked hard by a car. We had been playing ball in the street and a too-fast car roared around the corner and threw him fifty feet in the air where he landed on the lawn, unconscious and not moving, so we thought he must be dead. The man with the bad leg was there too, before we saw him come. No one knew what to do. The man was pushing down now on our poor friend's chest and breathing into his lungs a deep, full breath through the drool, until our friend shook a bit, coughed, and then opened his eyes, alive again, and ready to go.

Words for the Dancing Wu Li Masters

Everything wants to leave us behind, something you cannot know unless you're keeping up. All arguments are the same. All compromise is different. Why did the chicken cross the road? To avoid the politician. Nothing is faster than light and nothing leaves a black hole except what leaves it. Nothing else. Time is an invention the way space is real. We live in space but not in time. When their light reaches us, most of the stars have already died, murdered by space. Yet just when we believed that it was all moving away from us, someone else suggests otherwise, that it all could be coming back. The numbers are there, man. They may not be right, but the numbers are there.

Fishing in Hà Nội

I am not a young man. I know that. So when I fell down hard on the concrete bank of the small lake on Nguyễn Du, I didn't hesitate to take a young man's hand who wanted to help me up. I'd been trying to learn to fish Vietnamese style, and my line was hung up a few meters offshore. I took my shoes off, rolled up my jeans and began to wade into the water to try and dislodge my hook so I wouldn't lose it. I took one step onto the slippery bottom and fell on my ass in a splash. No one laughed except me. People came to help me. I was soaked from my waist down. Another man came to help with my hook and gave me some instructions on how to avoid getting caught up in the sharp rocks just off shore underwater. Someone else offered me a float to use, and someone else brought some bait. I have fished all of my life. I grew up on Lake Erie, and later in my life I fished the limestone creeks of central Pennsylvania for brown trout. My father taught me to fish at a place called hot waters when I was just big enough to hold the rod and cast, but today I had to learn all over again, from my Vietnamese friends, who were concerned that I struggled a bit, and wasn't catching any fish, and I want to speak to the solitary kindness of strangers I find here, who want to help you for no other reason than you need help. This is not complicated, I think.

Caged Bird in Hà Nội

Only a few meters from the sidewalk, and across the street from the park, I found a nest where a homeless person had spent the night. At the end of December, Hà Nội can be cold, so this person had dragged a large stump with broken branches sticking out from somewhere. Part of it he, or she, used as a bed over which some torn cloth had been spread, and part of it he, or she, burned, all night probably, to stay warm. The space was empty now but not abandoned. Whoever it was would be back, I was certain, because of how the blanket was spread so carefully over the cradle of branches, and how the smoke still rose from the dying fire. I thought about how comfortable I had been in my bed last night, my windows open to the cool air but my blanket cozy, and warm. I don't know why we all can't be warm when it's too cold outside to sleep. I don't know why there isn't enough of everything for everyone when there is so much for some. I thought about hanging around until someone returned, maybe trying to help them, but then I wouldn't know what to do. In the nearby lake old men fish with baited hooks, or jerk their treble hooks through the water, hoping to snag something. A woman sells tea from two thermos bottles and Thăng Longs by the cigarette, business as usual. Someone's caged bird sings.

Metaphysical There

The tree frog's two syllables rising from night trees sound exactly like a plea, or like a final question: *is it is it is it*, and it means oh what a night we inhabit together, hanging our songs out in the cool air like blessings on the doorframe.

Until I found my life there, I was afraid of the dark. Until it had hidden me from grave danger, I didn't know how close the embrace of night in all its splendor through which I could hear voices and footsteps but was never seen.

So now I haunt my own backyard in the pitch dark, only a neighbor's small light across the way. I am looking for something that isn't there.

Coffee in Hà Nội

Coffee here, especially on the street, is not a small matter whether you're alone or with friends. With friends, once you order, you share your news and gossip about who is not there. When you drink alone, you take your phone out, or read a newspaper or magazine. If you're having coffee with condensed milk and ice, *cà phê sữa đá*, then the first thing you do is stir the coffee rigorously to mix the condensed milk and coffee together. You also want the ice to chill the coffee, so you don't drink anything for at least the first ten minutes, although you are allowed to touch the glass, and to turn it in your hand while you look away. Once you finally allow yourself a sip of the cold and sweet coffee, it is only a very small sip, and you are quick to set the glass back down on the table and return to your phone, or to watching the traffic float past. If you are with friends then you want to be the slowest coffee drinker at the table. I'm not sure why. If you're alone, it's better to pace yourself with someone sitting nearby lest you drink too quickly, which is easy to do, especially if you're a gulping American. But not in Hà Nội. Your sips are far and few between, and if anything waits for you, it will have to keep waiting, because there is no rushing this ritual. Once I'd managed to stretch my coffee drinking into thirty minutes, my friends laughed at me and asked me why I was in such a rush. An hour is not a long time, necessarily, when you're sharing good coffee with friends on a busy street, the world in all its splendor spinning around you.

What I Learned from the Night Bird in Hà Nội

The first night I walked late around the lake on Nguyễn Du to help me find some peace before sleep, I was followed by a young woman who looked like a college student in the street lights. She was on the sidewalk, and I was walking parallel near the edge of the lake. There were only a few other people around, some late fishermen, snagging with their treble hooks, some lovers with nowhere else to go, sharing a bench, and this woman and me. She finally called out to me something I couldn't understand, and she crossed the way to join me near the lake. When she got closer she looked even younger than I had thought; she was a girl really, and I wondered why she was out so late and alone. She asked me then if I wanted her to go to my hotel, in English, and when I asked her why I would want her at my hotel, she said in English, *You know,* and laughed. I told her I didn't stay at a hotel. I thanked her for her offer and kept walking. She said she'd see me later and goodbye, and I watched her walk around the lake again, making that circle in the dark, hoping to find some business.

Several nights later I saw her again. This time she told me her name was Hơn, and that she was twenty-two years old, younger than both of my children. We didn't talk about what she was doing out there, but she did ask me where I was from and if I was married and if I spoke Vietnamese. She told me that strangers weren't always kind to her, even her customers, and that she was grateful for my kindness. I don't know much about this fucking life, why there's cruelty and disrespect. By nineteen Hơn had two children and neither father offered any financial support. She was only trying to care for them now, using the delicate tools of her body to make enough money. I walk often around the lake. Each time I see her she looks more tired and weary. I offer her money which she won't accept, but she agrees to let me buy her lunch one day. She is beautiful in the early afternoon light, in spite of how worn down the world has made her, and she tells me proudly about the new clothes she just bought for her daughters. I don't know much about this life, or about what things finally come to, if anything at all.

Blood, for X.

I'm inside of my mine now where the river's been blown out, a wall of blood cascading just behind me so I run fast; even after everything, I stay ahead of the wall of blood. I know not to ask questions about the origin of pain, or about the screams that tear the flawless sky to shreds right before our eyes. I know that much.

A thing that hunts us all keeps us apart; it wants to kill as many as it can. You'll walk along the lake without my hand around your hand, your voice around my heart; you'll walk alone for this is how it is, and I won't pray for any god to save us from ourselves, but I will hold the whole of you inside of me, where you have found your way, the blood a darkened purple wave not here, not far away.

Outside Quảng Trị City, 1968

I'm watching out the window the cat stalk the robin pulling up worms don't say a word so I must be complicit when you fire into the dark trees when you fire round after round into the dark trees without knowing who hides there until we stop.

Mưa Xuân

Spring rain is that fine mist you feel fall across your face like fine lace, no room for your umbrella to pass on the crowded street, so I keep it closed, my shirt already soaked through, beads of sweat small pearls down my face. *Mưa Xuân,* my friend says as we make our way down the crowded street, *spring rain,* and the diversity of the sensuous is unlike any metaphor; you have to feel the waves of history vibrate through you, before you know anything.

From a History of Many Lives

When she stops talking, the blackness of the unlit night begins to seep in upon them. She can feel the blackness move over them like a cloud in the rainy season, and with it, the blackness brings a quiet that is the quiet between things: between morning and night, between one heart beating for another, between the kiss and the last breath. She holds the hand of her brother, lover, and squeezes until he squeezes back. She closes her eyes and lets the blackness, which feels as if it has come to them from somewhere far away, overtake her completely, until they are engulfed in the swirling black, as in a flooded river; not drowning, but swept away, on a path the wind makes with its voice.

Acknowledgments

The author is grateful to editors of the following publications in which these pieces first appeared:

The American Journal of Poetry: "The Man in the Chair," "The Problem with Shapes in the Night Trees," "Black Swans in the Garden of Perfect Splendor," "Sometimes How It Feels," "Miami Nights, "Draft of Final Chorus I," "Draft of Final Chorus II," "This Back-Porch Rocker My Prison," "Liquor Was Involved," "Clinical Notes Number Ninety-One," "Lost," "Homewood Nineteen Fifty Something," "War Story," "The Still Unravished Bryn of Quietude," and "Après Flashback for My Good Doctor";

Consequence: "Thăng Long," "Bad Day," "Sutra," and "Standing Before the Arch of Triumph in Bucharest, I Think of Lorain, Ohio and of Quảng Trị Province, Việt Nam";

Here: A Poetry Journal: "Drawing I," "Sutra";

Juxtaprose: "Tale of the Tortoise";

Literary Matters: "Metaphysical There," "Caged Bird in Hà Nội" and "Outside Quảng Trị City, 1968";

Pedestal: "Out Here" and "Blood, for X.";

Plume: "Clinical Notes Number Ninety-Two";

TriQuarterly: "Wade Park VA," "Watching My Great-Uncle Shave, Johnstown, PA, Circa 1954," "At a Car Wash in Little Rock," "Tell Them Everything," and "Lost in Beijing."

"The People Have Spoken and They Are Ugly," "Draft of Final Chorus I," "Draft of Final Chorus II," and "War Story" originally appeared in the anthology *The Mighty Stream: Poems in Celebration of Martin Luther King*, edited by Carolyn Forché and Jackie Kay.

"Black Swans in the Garden of Perfect Splendor" and "Frog Melody" originally appeared in *Waxwing Triptych for Peace, No. 4* (Ireland), edited by John Dean.

I am grateful for the support of my editor, Peter Conners, for seeing the prose in this book and for his wicked good eye, and for the staff at BOA for their many contributions. Thanks also for the friendship of my colleagues at Appalachian State University where I was able to begin this manuscript in my beautiful mountain home in Blowing Rock, particularly Bruce Dick and Joseph Bathanti, and for the attention of several kind people who took the time to read this manuscript in progress and offer advice and encouragement, including Kevin Bowen, Andrew Weigl, Diane Vreuls, Stuart Friebert, Xia Lu, and for the amazingly right-on editorial work of Reginald Gibbons, my sweet friend, true mentor, and rigorous editor for many years, without whose help and support I could not have done this work. Special thanks to Nguyễn Phan Quế Mai for her expertise in help with the Vietnamese names, and for providing the full diacritics, without which the words would be meaningless. We provide these accent marks here as a sign of respect for the Vietnamese culture.

About the Author

Bruce Weigl's most recent poetry collection is *On the Shores of Welcome Home,* which won the Isabella Gardner Award for Poetry and was published by BOA Editions, Ltd. in 2019. Previously he published *The Abundance of Nothing* (TriQuarterly Books), one of three finalists for the Pulitzer Prize in Poetry in 2013; a memoir, *The Circle of Hanh* (Grove Press, 2000); as well as more than twenty-five other works of poetry, essays, and translations from the Vietnamese and the Romanian. He lives in Oberlin, Ohio, and in Hà Nội, Việt Nam. His work has been translated and widely published in Việt Nam.

BOA Editions, Ltd. American Reader Series

Colophon

BOA Editions, Ltd., a not-for-profit publisher of poetry and other literary works, fosters readership and appreciation of contemporary literature. By identifying, cultivating, and publishing both new and established poets and selecting authors of unique literary talent, BOA brings high-quality literature to the public. Support for this effort comes from the sale of its publications, grant funding, and private donations.

The publication of this book is made possible, in part, by the special support of the following individuals:

Anonymous (x2)
Nelson Adrian Blish
Gary & Gwen Conners
Charles & Danielle Coté
The Chris Dahl & Ruth Rowse Charitable Fund
The David J. Fraher Charitable Fund,
in memory of A. Poulin, Jr.
Bonnie Garner
Reginald Gibbons
Margaret Heminway
Grant Holcomb
Kathleen C. Holcombe
Nora A. Jones
Paul LaFerriere & Dorrie Parini
Jack & Gail Langerak
Tony Leuzzi
Peter & Phyllis Makuck
Joe McElveney
Sherry Phillips & Richard Margolis Donor Advised Fund
Boo Poulin
Elizabeth Spenst
David St. John
Deborah Ronnen
William Waddell & Linda Rubel